T0013254

TINY JOYS

Also by Katie Vaz
My Life in Plants
The Escape Manual for Introverts
Make Yourself Cozy

Coloring Books
Cottagecore Galore
Life with Plants
Don't Worry, Eat Cake

TINY JOYS

a guide to embracing
your inner
coastal grandmother

KATIE VAZ

Andrews McMeel
PUBLISHING®

Tiny Joys copyright © 2023 by Katie Vaz. All rights reserved.
Printed in China. No part of this book may be used or reproduced
in any manner whatsoever without written permission
except in the case of reprints in the context of reviews.

Andrews McMeel Publishing
a division of Andrews McMeel Universal
1130 Walnut Street, Kansas City, Missouri 64106

www.andrewsmcmeel.com

23 24 25 26 27 SDB 10 9 8 7 6 5 4 3 2 1

ISBN: 978-1-5248-8346-1

Library of Congress Control Number: 2022950395

Editor: Patty Rice
Art Director: Diane Marsh
Production Editor: Elizabeth A. Garcia
Production Manager: Tamara Haus

ATTENTION: SCHOOLS AND BUSINESSES
Andrews McMeel books are available at quantity discounts with
bulk purchase for educational, business, or sales promotional use.
For information, please e-mail the Andrews McMeel Publishing
Special Sales Department: sales@amuniversal.com.

For Tater,
who always reminds me
to appreciate the tiny joys in life

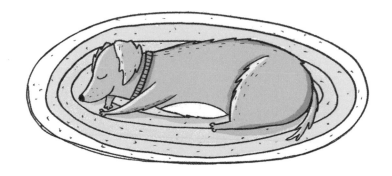

WELCOME

This book is an illustrated guide that celebrates the tiny joys of life. Equal parts inspirational guide, gratitude journal, and activity book, it's inspired by the lovely "coastal grandmother" aesthetic made popular on social media by influencer Lex Nicoleta, who is credited for coining the phrase. "Coastal grandmother" is an aspirational lifestyle that celebrates the daydream of what it would be like to live on the coast: outfits of cream-colored sweaters and breezy linen pants, dreamy kitchens full of the scents of freshly baked croissants and the sounds of Harry Connick Jr., mornings spent gardening or shopping at farmers markets, and evenings spent sipping crisp white wine while curled up with a favorite book on your porch. Think Ina Garten, any 2000s movie with Diane Keaton, or any Nancy Meyers movie set (those kitchens!).

I loved the idea of incorporating the essence of that into my own life. In fact, I'd already been a fan of Ina since I was about twelve! As I dove into the world of "coastal grandmother," I realized there was something even deeper about the aesthetic that resonated with me, even though I don't live on the beach, I'm not a grandmother, and I'm definitely not a rich divorcée like Meryl Streep in *It's Complicated*. I don't think you have to be any of those things either to appreciate the accompanying mindset that comes with this lifestyle.

To me, being a coastal grandmother is about creating a good life for oneself, with an emphasis on finding joy in the simple and good things in life and making even the most ordinary of days feel special. It's about savoring life, aging peacefully, appreciating good food, wearing comfortable clothes and feeling comfortable in your body, spending time in nature, enjoying company but also delighting in solitude, creating a home with lived-in charm, valuing leisure and rest, and noticing the tiny joys in your life.

Inside this book, you'll find ideas for how to incorporate this luxuriously simple lifestyle into your day-to-day life, as well as space for you to add your own ideas about joy through journaling or drawing. I hope these pages inspire you to embrace your inner coastal grandmother and celebrate the joys of a life lived at ease.

THIS IS YOUR LIFE
and you are
ALLOWED
to enjoy
LIVING
IT.
PERMISSION SLIP
Enjoy your one, precious life.

A COASTAL GRANDMOTHER CHECKLIST

Je prends un pain au chocolat, s'il vous plaît.

PAIN AU CHOCOLAT

barefoot Contessa
how easy is that?

HEIRLOOM TOMATO
Cherokee Purple

the Holiday

THE NECESSITIES:

- ☐ breezy, comfortable clothing
- ☐ a love of any Nancy Meyers movie
- ☐ basic French language skills (probably food-based)
- ☐ a garden full of heirloom varieties
- ☐ an appreciation of good wine
- ☐ farmers market vendors who know your name
- ☐ fresh pastries in your kitchen
- ☐ Ina Garten cookbook collection
- ☐ a home filled with the warmth and essence of you

WHAT DOES JOY MEAN TO YOU?

_____
_____
_____
_____
_____

Does it remind you
of a particular place?

What does it feel like?

Does joy
have a flavor
or scent?

What does it
sound like to
you?

DESCRIBE YOUR FAVORITE TINY JOYS. WHY DO THEY FILL YOUR HEART WITH WARMTH?

_____

_____

_____

_____

_____

_____

_____

_____

_____

_____

5

puff pastry cheese danishes

cinnamony coffee cake

citrusy loaf cake

glazed baked berry donuts

START THE DAY BY
BAKING A TREAT YOU CAN
ENJOY LATER THAT MORNING
WITH A WARM DRINK.

fluffy fruit-studded muffins

FILL A FEW VASES WITH FRESHLY CUT
FLOWERS FROM YOUR GARDEN TO BRING
THE OUTDOORS IN TO YOU.

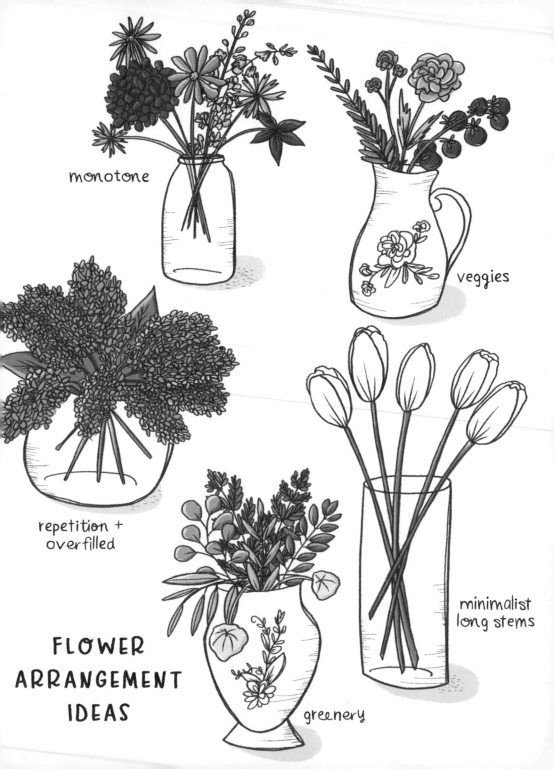

monotone

veggies

repetition +
overfilled

greenery

minimalist
long stems

FLOWER
ARRANGEMENT
IDEAS

heirloom varieties

COASTAL GRANDMOTHER GARDEN STARTER PACK

for decadent bouquets

tomatoes on a trellis

luscious blooms like peonies

vining garden roses

perennials that attract bees and butterflies

lettuce greens

for fresh salads anytime

organized raised beds

garden dining area

picket fences

keeps the garden tidy

hydrangeas, of course

a walk with a friend

a local barre class

REJUVENATING EXERCISE IDEAS TO ADD SOME JOY TO YOUR MORNING

yoga on your deck

Maybe a peaceful rainstorm...

WHAT TYPES OF SOUNDS BRING JOY TO YOU?

...or a cozy crackling fire?

petting a furry friend

JOY CAN COME FROM TACTILE SENSATIONS, TOO. WHAT FEELS GOOD TO YOU?

the refreshing coolness of lake water

luxurious fabrics like cashmere

kneading soft
bread dough

a loving
embrace

digging your hands
into earthy garden soil

the comfort of
wrapping your hands
around a warm mug

Is there another sensation
that brings you joy?

draw
it here
↙

WHAT JOYS DID YOU FIND TODAY? DID YOU NOTICE THEM IN THE MOMENT OR AFTERWARDS?

MIX + MATCH

clothes

ribbed
turtleneck

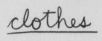
striped sweater

with
pockets,
← of course

flowy
midi
dress

linen tank top

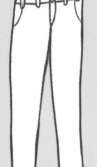

straight-leg jeans

white
button-up

palazzo pants

pleated ankle
pants

a neutral long
cardigan

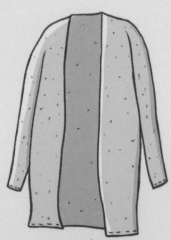

accessories

floppy sun hat

classic red lipstick

canvas tote

silk scarf

timeless jewelry

your favorite sunglasses

farmers market basket

leather loafers

shoes

white tennis shoes

slides

= AN OUTFIT THAT FEELS COMFORTABLE AND POLISHED

INVEST IN A GOOD WHITE BUTTON-DOWN SHIRT.

THERE ARE SO MANY WAYS YOU CAN WEAR IT!

underneath a cardigan

tied with a knot

open over
another shirt

tucked in

loosely
buttoned

23

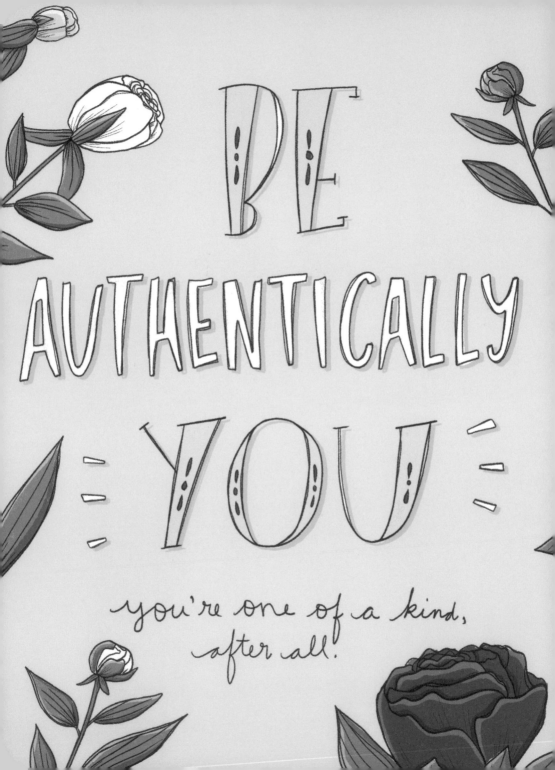

BE
AUTHENTICALLY
YOU

you're one of a kind,
after all!

SEEK THE FREEDOM OF
LIVING AS YOUR TRUE SELF
(AND NOT CARING WHAT
OTHERS THINK).

WHAT MAKES YOU
"YOU"?

_____

_____

_____

_____

WHAT BRINGS YOU JOY
WHEN NO ONE ELSE IS
PAYING ATTENTION?

_____

_____

_____

_____

OH, THE SIMPLE JOY OF REALLY, REALLY GOOD BREAD.

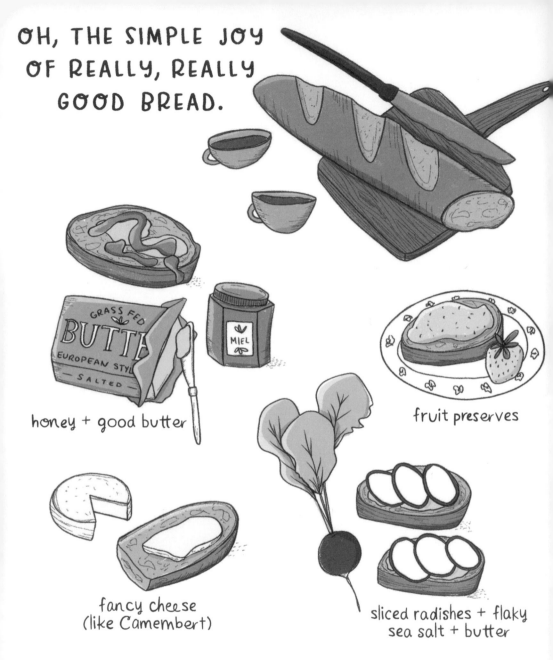

honey + good butter

fruit preserves

fancy cheese
(like Camembert)

sliced radishes + flaky
sea salt + butter

GRAB A FRESH BAGUETTE AND TRY SOME OF THESE TOPPINGS.

HAVE AN OUTDOOR TEA PARTY
WITH FRIENDS.

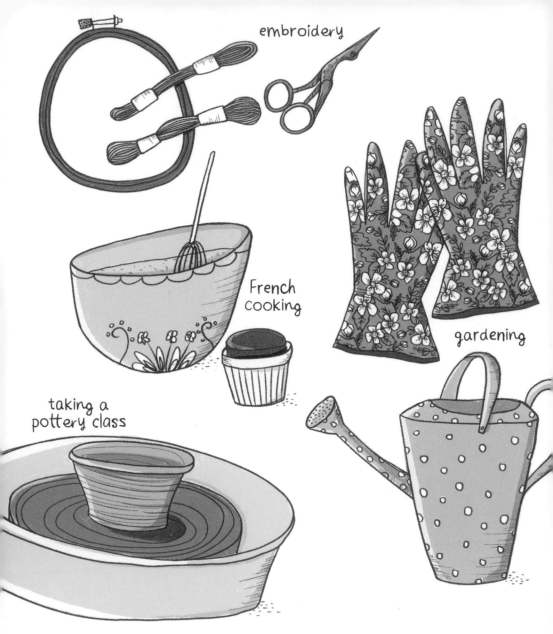

embroidery

French cooking

gardening

taking a pottery class

INSTEAD OF SCROLLING, HOW ABOUT USING THAT TIME TO TRY OUT A NEW HOBBY?

add flair to home decor

makes for a special gift, too!

ADD EMBROIDERY TO MAKE YOUR THINGS FEEL A LITTLE MORE PERSONALIZED AND SPECIAL.

add an heirloom feel to cloth napkins

Bon appétit

dress up a plain sweater

KEEP COOKIE DOUGH
IN YOUR FREEZER FOR
FRESH-BAKED COOKIES
AT ANY TIME.

earl grey +
lavender

rosemary shortbread

classic peanut
butter

chocolate chunk +
flaky sea salt

REFRESHING DRINKS TO BRIGHTEN YOUR DAY

crisp white wine

a botanical
lavender lemonade

iced tea with fresh mint

cucumber-infused
water

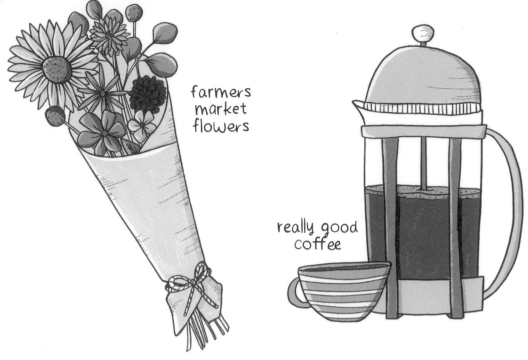

farmers market flowers

really good coffee

TREAT YOURSELF TO SOME SIMPLE, BUT VERY INDULGENT, LUXURIES

high-quality dark chocolate

VELVETY DARK CHOCOLATE 88%

a favorite candle

AMALFI COAST

BAKERY SPECIAL pistachio croissants

fresh pastries

WHAT ARE SOME OTHER LITTLE LUXURIES THAT COULD BRIGHTEN YOUR DAY?

_____

_____

_____

_____

_____

_____

FILL IN WITH TINY JOYS YOU CAN INCORPORATE INTO ANY DAY

_____ is an easy, nourishing meal I know how to make.

Watching _____ makes me feel content.

_____ is a treat that tastes like pure happiness to me.

_____ is a book I love escaping into.

Listening to _____ always makes me want to sway or dance.

_____ is my favorite way to move my body and feel alive.

WHAT OTHER JOYFUL ACTIVITIES CAN YOU ADD TO ANY ORDINARY DAY?

_____

_____

_____

_____

_____

_____

SAVOR THE exciting DAYS. the ORDINARY DAYS. and EVERYTHING IN BETWEEN.

IF LIFE FEELS PARTICULARLY HECTIC, TRY ADDING "SAVOR" DATES TO YOUR CALENDAR, JUST LIKE ANY OTHER APPOINTMENT.

Savoring is about recognizing, appreciating, and absorbing good feelings as they happen.

SEND A HANDWRITTEN LETTER TO A FRIEND. HOW CAN YOU ELEVATE IT AND MAKE IT MORE SPECIAL?

elegant calligraphy

include a happy photograph

decorate the envelope

include pressed flowers from your garden

You're invited!
A PARTY TO CELEBRATE
my blooming hydrangeas
7 p.m.
Friday

DON'T SAVE CELEBRATIONS FOR THE BIG MILESTONES OF LIFE. CELEBRATE THE LITTLE STUFF, TOO.

Happy Tuesday!

COOKIE CAKE SHOP

Yay!

YOU FINISHED THAT TO-DO LIST

Y A Y

WHAT OTHER ORDINARY THINGS WOULD BE FUN TO CELEBRATE?

ALWAYS have something TO LOOK forward to.

THESE CAN BE BIG THINGS LIKE VACATIONS AS WELL AS TINY THINGS THAT HAPPEN IN DAILY LIFE.

↑ it's the anticipation that creates joy!

Maybe it's a European trip you'll go on in a couple of years...

...or next year's garden...

...or the tasty homemade granola you'll have at breakfast tomorrow.

WHAT ARE SOME THINGS YOU'RE LOOKING FORWARD TO?

California beach house

oceanfront home in New England

WHERE WOULD YOUR DREAM VACATION HOME BE LOCATED?

charming cottage in the French countryside

seaside Italian villa

or maybe somewhere else?

draw it here ↙

44

WOULD YOU RATHER...

☐ eat pain au chocolat   OR   eat a profiterole ☐

☐ drink strawberry sangria   OR   drink a strawberry milkshake ☐

☐ walk on a beach   OR   walk in a botanical garden ☐

☐ have a dinner party   OR   eat dinner alone while ☐
watching a favorite movie

☐ grow hydrangeas   OR   grow peonies ☐

☐ make homemade   OR   make an heirloom ☐
tomato soup   tomato tart

☐ vacation in Cape Cod   OR   vacation in Paris ☐

HAVE YOU EVER WANTED TO TAKE A FRENCH LANGUAGE CLASS?

WHAT WOULD YOU DO IN PARIS WITH YOUR NEW LANGUAGE SKILLS?

PALAIS ROYAL →

LES ARTS DÉCORATIFS →

MUSÉE DU LOUVRE →

← ÉGLISE ST. GERMAIN

BOULANGERIE

MERCI BEAUCOUP
Thank you very much

BONJOUR
Hello

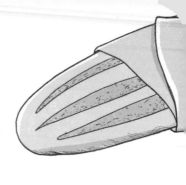

S'IL VOUS PLAÎT
Please

OUI
Yes

AU REVOIR
Goodbye

NON
No

COMMENT ALLEZ-VOUS?
How are you?

THINK OF THE BEST VACATION OR TRIP YOU'VE EVER TAKEN. LET THE MEMORIES WARM YOU.

HOW CAN YOU INCORPORATE THE JOY FROM THE TRIP INTO YOUR EVERYDAY LIFE?

re-creating a delicious meal you had at a memorable restaurant

AIR FRANCE Boarding Pass
3 JANUARY
GATE A21
ORIGIN: NEW YORK
DESTINATION: PARIS
GATE A21
SEAT 14A
JFK CDG

PASSPORT

ROSÉ

re-creating something that felt luxurious, like really fluffy bedding from a great hotel you stayed at

crafting with a souvenir you brought home

incorporate a daily ritual, like sitting down and enjoying an espresso and a pastry in the afternoon

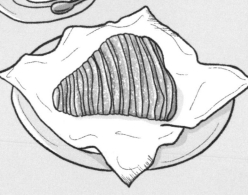

PLAN A RELAXING PICNIC WITH YOUR FAVORITE PEOPLE.

WHAT WOULD YOU LIKE TO BRING?

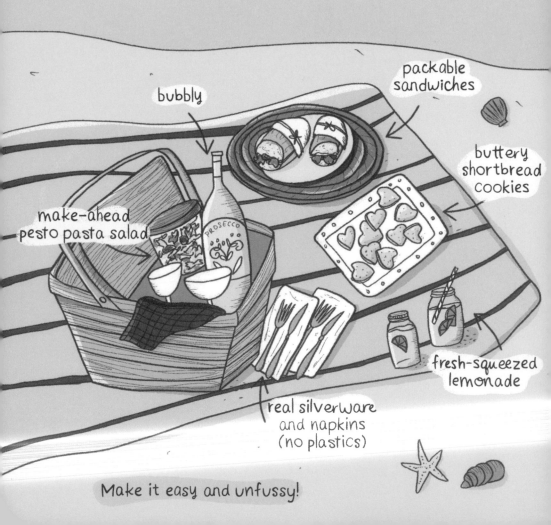

packable
sandwiches

bubbly

buttery
shortbread
cookies

make-ahead
pesto pasta salad

PROSECCO

fresh-squeezed
lemonade

real silverware
and napkins
(no plastics)

Make it easy and unfussy!

TRY WEARING SOMETHING JOYFUL TO BRING HAPPINESS TO MUNDANE ACTIVITIES.

wear your favorite colors to doctor appointments

paint a happy manicure for a tedious or stressful work meeting

wear happy jewelry while doing chores

oh the SWEETNESS of a MELTY ICE CREAM CONE

WHICH FLAVORS TASTE LIKE JOY TO YOU?

ADD RAINBOW SPRINKLES TO INFUSE INSTANT JOY.

breakfast treats

a retro milkshake

dainty pastries

cozy hot chocolate

a gift for you

You can even try making homemade sprinkles to give as a gift!

EASY WAYS TO ADD COASTAL
GRANDMOTHER VIBES TO ANY MEALTIME

sit at an actual table and add tactile features like soft tablecloths or cloth napkins

use tableware that looks joyful to you

REIGNITE THE JOY OF EATING BY PRACTICING MINDFULNESS AT MEALTIMES.

avoid multitasking while eating, if possible

savor your food slowly and truly notice the flavors and textures

MONDAY

Schedule

12 lunch break

55

SIMPLE WAYS TO ENHANCE THE FLAVORS OF YOUR MEALS

chopped herbs

a dollop of crème fraîche

CRÈME FRAÎCHE

these should complement the flavors of the dish (not overpower)

a splash of red wine vinegar

RED WINE VINEGAR

citrus zest

but always go with what you like best!

flaky sea salt

grated cheese

SIMPLE GARNISHES TO MAKE ANY DISH PRETTIER

a sprig or two
of fresh herbs

lemon
slices

nuts and
seeds

edible
flowers

*like
pansies*

*or
chamomile*

balsamic
glaze

makes your kitchen smell so cozy!

SIMPLE AND GOOD FOOD TO MAKE IN YOUR DUTCH OVEN

no-knead bread

a whole roast chicken

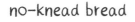

one-pot pasta with fresh veggies

something that can deliciously simmer for hours

a hearty stew

MIX + MATCH

food and drinks

comforting pasta

veggie-packed soup

roasted skillet chicken

fresh garden salad

fresh-squeezed lemonade

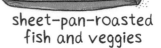
sheet-pan-roasted fish and veggies

favorite sparkling water

fancy cocktail

after-dinner activities

reading in bed with a hot cup of tea

catching up with a dear friend

after-dinner stroll

curling up on the couch with a classic movie

= A RELAXING FRIDAY EVENING

ADD COASTAL GRANDMOTHER AMBIENCE WITH THIS PLAYLIST IDEA

1. Sunday Kind of Love by Etta James

2. C'est Si Bon by Eartha Kitt

3. A Wink and a Smile by Harry Connick Jr.

4. This Will Be (An Everlasting Love) by Natalie Cole

5. Come Away With Me by Norah Jones

6. Cheek To Cheek by Ella Fitzgerald + Louis Armstrong

7. Mama Said by The Shirelles

8. Coming Home by Leon Bridges

9. L'ombre et la lumière by Coralie Clement

10. You Send Me by Aretha Franklin

11. Tears Dry On Their Own by Amy Winehouse

12. La Vie en rose by Edith Piaf

13. Stand by Me by Otis Redding

14. Isn't She Lovely by Stevie Wonder

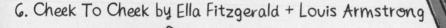

SIMPLE PASTA IDEAS FOR QUICK AND DELICIOUS WEEKNIGHT DINNERS

cacio e pepe (means "cheese and pepper" in Italian)

kind of like a grown-up mac + cheese!

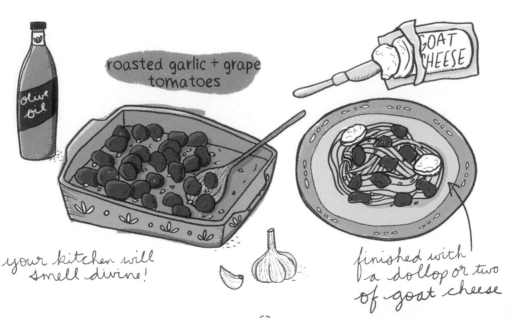

roasted garlic + grape tomatoes

olive oil

GOAT CHEESE

your kitchen will smell divine!

finished with a dollop or two of goat cheese

eggplant arrabiata

a spicy sauce (arrabiata means "angry" in Italian)

Crushed tomatoes

PASTA SAUCE

crushed tomatoes or your favorite jarred pasta sauce will work!

CRUSHED RED PEPPER FLAKES

pesto pasta salad

homemade pesto is great, but you can easily swap in store-bought if you're short on time!

CILIEGINE

with mozzarella balls and fresh cherry tomatoes

Turn the page for an easy pesto recipe you can make any time of year!

63

KALE & WALNUT pesto recipe

bold, bright, and garlicky!

Great on your favorite pasta...

...or on toast with a fried egg...

a quick and easy lunch!

...and even on homemade pizza!

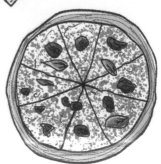

YOU'LL NEED:

2 cups torn kale leaves

i like tuscan kale here, but curly kale works, too!

make sure to trim away the stems

juice of 1 lemon

4 cloves of garlic, chopped

use less if you'd like a more mild flavor

OLIVE OIL

1/4 cup chopped walnuts

1/4 cup olive oil

1/2 cup grated pecorino romano cheese

sea salt

sea salt + black pepper to taste

DIRECTIONS:

Add kale leaves, garlic, walnuts, and lemon juice to a food processor. Pulse until the kale looks finely chopped. Add olive oil, grated cheese, and a pinch of salt and pepper (add more or less to your taste). Grind until the mixture is well-combined. Use as a sauce or a spread.

taking a warm bath

tending to your plants

AFTER A STRESSFUL DAY, WHAT'S YOUR FAVORITE WAY TO DECOMPRESS AND ADD MORE JOY TO YOUR EVENING?

POWER OFF

turning off your phone

Lemon bars

trying out a new recipe

TREAT YOURSELF TO THE JOY
OF BEING IN BED EARLY.

soft music

a good novel

herbal tea

aromatherapy

furry company

soft lighting

draw
another
bedtime
tiny joy

IMAGINE A LOVELY DAY WITH ABSOLUTELY NO OBLIGATIONS. HOW WOULD YOU SPEND IT?

_____

_____

_____

_____

_____

_____

_____

COULD YOU RE-CREATE SOME OF
THIS MAGIC ON EVEN THE BUSIEST
OF DAYS? WHAT SMALL JOYS
COULD YOU INCORPORATE?

_____

_____

_____

_____

_____

_____

_____

MIX + MATCH
yummy foods + drinks

dutch baby pancake with fresh berries

hot chocolate

raspberry sweet rolls

mimosas

BUBBLY

fresh fruit

croque monsieur

omelette and greens

savory quiche

big carafe of hot coffee

SUGAR

CREAM

special touches

linen napkins

cake stands or tiered serving platters

your favorite dishes (they don't have to match!)

pain au chocolat

blackberry lavender scones

pretty labels

fresh flowers or potted plants

= A LOVELY SATURDAY BRUNCH

GRAB A TOTE OR BASKET AND VISIT YOUR LOCAL FARMERS MARKET.

HERE ARE SOME IDEAS OF WHAT TO SHOP FOR BASED ON THE SEASON.

shopping list

rhubarb

Spring

strawberries

scallions

Shop local

asparagus

spinach

radishes

fiddleheads

snap peas

peaches

summer

heirloom tomatoes

corn

garlic

plums

blueberries

garlic scapes

summer squash

cherries

cucumbers

watermelon

fall

apples

pumpkins

beets

winter squash

pears

cranberries

DIFFERENT IDEAS FOR USING FRESH HEIRLOOM TOMATOES

(from the garden or farmers market)

← always with white bread and mayo

sauteed with garlic and basil

a classic tomato sandwich

on crusty bread with pesto

with fresh mozzarella →

olive oil

caprese salad

BALSAMIC VINEGAR

simply cut into wedges with a bit of flaky sea salt

HOW ELSE DO YOU LIKE TO EAT FRESH TOMATOES?

EDIBLE HOMEMADE GIFTS ARE A
THOUGHTFUL TOUCH TO ANY OCCASION.

GROWING OLDER means you're GETTING TO KNOW YOURSELF better.

WHAT ARE SOME THINGS YOU ENJOY MORE NOW THAN YOU DID 10 YEARS AGO?

_____

_____

_____

_____

_____

_____

_____

_____

_____

maybe some of your favorite wine, too

a great way to use up farmers market produce

salty cornichons and olives

grilled or toasted bread

hummus with a drizzle of olive oil

your favorite cheese

ripe summer fruit

crunchy veggies

fresh dip, like pesto yogurt

"grazing boards" are great for company, too!

HAVE A "SNACK DINNER" FOR A RELAXED, PRODUCE-FILLED MEAL.

OR FOR SOMETHING EASY AND SWEET AFTER DINNER, TRY A DESSERT BOARD!

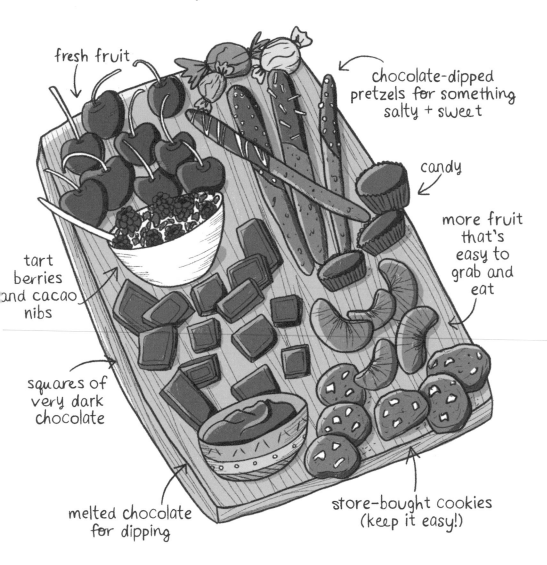

fresh fruit

chocolate-dipped pretzels for something salty + sweet

candy

more fruit that's easy to grab and eat

tart berries and cacao nibs

squares of very dark chocolate

melted chocolate for dipping

store-bought cookies (keep it easy!)

perfect for those times you don't have time to bake or you don't want to turn on the oven!

WHAT ARE SOME GOOD SCENTS TO YOU?

a pie baking in your oven

salty ocean air

Is there another scent that brings joy to you?

draw it here ↙

fragrant flowers in your garden

laundry that's been hung to dry outside

WEEKEND BAKING PROJECT IDEAS

bagels

pain au chocolat

macarons

French apple tart

Charlotte cake

madeleines

picking out a recipe during the week gives you something to look forward to!

MIX + MATCH
NOURISHING SALADS

greens

mustard greens

spinach

kale

romaine lettuce

baby arugula

stars of the show
(veggies + fruits + proteins)

roasted sweet potatoes

sliced apples

marinated tofu

roasted beets

sliced pears

grilled chicken

strawberry slices

toppings

avocado

roasted chickpeas

pepitas

pomegranate seeds

olives

candied walnuts

feta cheese

goat cheese

sliced almonds

dried cranberries

then add your favorite dressing!

Combo ideas

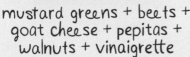

mustard greens + beets + goat cheese + pepitas + walnuts + vinaigrette

kale + sweet potatoes + sliced apples + dried cranberries + honey mustard dressing

spinach + pears + feta + pomegranate seeds + sliced almonds + drizzle of balsamic glaze

IDEAS FOR COOKBOOKS TO TRY

modern Comfort food
ina garten

basically anything by ina garten will give coastal grandmother vibes!

a classic!

Mastering the Art of French Cooking
julia child

FRUIT DESSERTS
martha stewart

just one example, but she has many!

THE TUCCI COOKBOOK
stanley tucci

a "coastal grandfather"

the SILVERPALATE COOKBOOK
julia rosso
sheila lukins

has great entertaining ideas, too!

SIMPLE + ELEGANT DESSERTS FOR BUSY WEEKNIGHTS

fresh berries with crème fraîche and a drizzle of honey

CRÈME FRAÎCHE

an easy way to showcase your farmers market haul →

FROZEN PUFF PASTRY

French palmier cookies

frozen puff pastry + butter + sugar (that's it!)

BOURBON CARAMEL VANILLA ice cream

cookie ice cream sandwiches

the cookie bakery

MOLASSES

Use store-bought and whatever flavors you prefer!

LEMONS CAN ADD A DOSE OF SUNSHINE AND JOY TO A RAINY DAY. TRY MAKING THESE CHEERFUL LEMON IDEAS.

pasta al limone

a cheerful lemon bundt cake

lemon, cinnamon, and rosemary stovetop potpourri

HOMEMADE limoncello

homemade limoncello to give as a gift

preserved lemons

preserved lemons

HOST A BOOK CLUB WITH FRIENDS.

with soft and comfy places to sit

a book you couldn't put down!

and good wine

and delicious snacks

+ enlightening conversation with friends

WHICH BOOKS WOULD YOU SUGGEST?

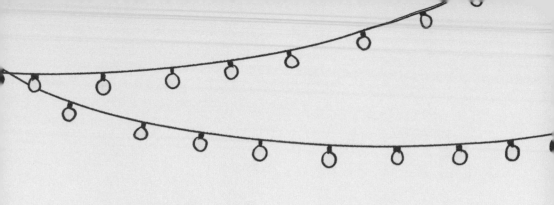

SHARE AN AL FRESCO
CHEESE BOARD WITH A FRIEND.

MIX + MATCH

breakfast

fresh blueberry
pancakes

yogurt with
homemade
granola

cappuccino

jasmine green tea

soft scrambled
eggs with crusty
bread

outfits

soft cardigan

striped
button-up
shirt

breezy dress

linen
pants

straw hat

94

activities

hunt for cheery vases and
jars at an antique shop

buy a croissant
or two at a
local bakery

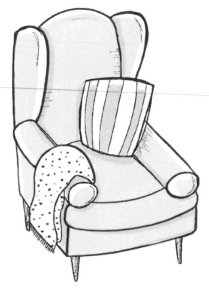

read a good book in
your favorite chair

tend to your flower
garden

= A VERY GOOD SUNDAY MORNING

vintage books

cute tea kettles

YOU DON'T NEED A BIG BUDGET TO ADD COASTAL GRANDMOTHER VIBES TO YOUR HOME.

wine and coupe glasses

vintage ginger jars

weathered and worn add charm!

high-quality French cookware

candlesticks

THESE ARE SOME THINGS YOU COULD FIND SECONDHAND.

cashmere sweaters

wicker baskets

KNOW WHAT you VALUE MOST.

WHAT MAKES LIFE FEEL MEANINGFUL TO YOU?

_____

_____

_____

_____

HOW CAN YOU PRIORITIZE THESE IN YOUR LIFE?

_____

_____

_____

_____

WHEN YOU KNOW WHAT IS IMPORTANT TO YOU, THERE IS MORE SPACE FOR JOY!

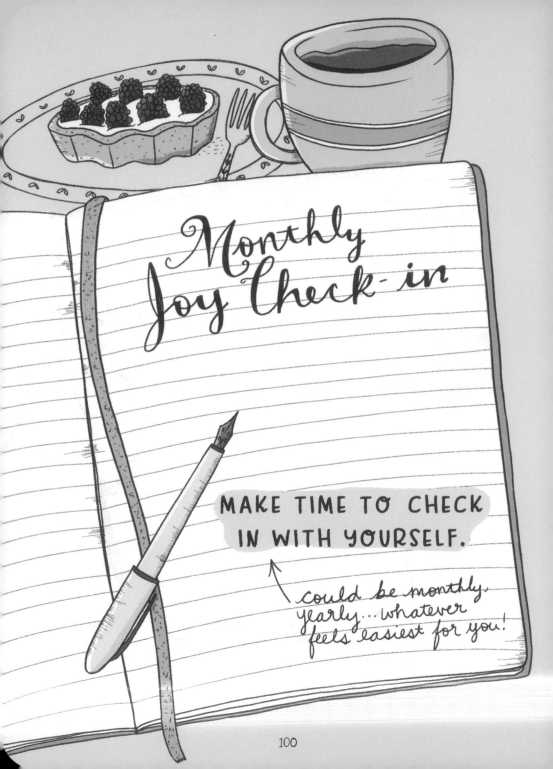

Monthly Joy Check-in

MAKE TIME TO CHECK IN WITH YOURSELF.

could be monthly, yearly...whatever feels easiest for you!

WHAT SOURCES OF HAPPINESS ARE CURRENTLY IN MY LIFE?

_____

_____

WHO ADDS THE MOST JOY TO MY LIFE?

_____

_____

IS THERE ANYTHING DEPLETING MY HAPPINESS THAT I HAVE CONTROL OVER?

_____

_____

WHAT CAN I DO TO FEEL MORE JOY BY MY NEXT CHECK-IN?

_____

_____

wrapping gifts
really nicely

maybe a
velvet ribbon

crisp butcher paper

THINGS THAT SEEM
A LITTLE "EXTRA"
BUT MAKE THE
ORDINARY FEEL
MORE SPECIAL

hydrating
avocado
EYE CREAM

Radient
Tinted
moisturizer

investing in good-quality
skincare/makeup

adds a warm
nuttiness

using brown butter
in recipes

especially good
in cookies!

travel memories

artwork that you like

favorite books

precious photos

DECORATE YOUR SHELVES WITH THINGS THAT MAKE YOUR HEART HAPPY.

favorite knick-knacks

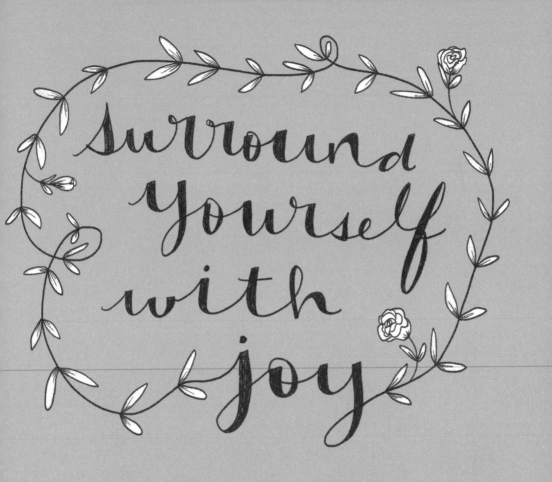

surround yourself with joy

SEE AND ENJOY YOUR BELONGINGS, RATHER THAN HIDING THEM AWAY OR SAVING THEM FOR "SPECIAL OCCASIONS."

fresh flowers, of course

ceramic vases

antique jars

vintage mirrors

personal touches

like your favorite family photographs

aim to fill your home with things that you feel emotionally connected to (don't worry about perfection)

THIS OR THAT

WHICH FEELS MORE JOYFUL TO YOU?

☐ board games on a rainy day   OR   outdoor yard games in the sunshine ☐

☐ the thrill of traveling to a new place   OR   the thrill of coming home and sleeping in your own bed ☐

☐ barefoot in the sand   OR   barefoot in the cool grass ☐

☐ book club with friends   OR   movie night with friends ☐

☐ make homemade pasta   OR   make homemade sourdough bread ☐

☐ picnic at the beach   OR   picnic at a park ☐

PUT ON A LUSH, WARM SWEATER AND HAVE A MORNING DRINK OUTSIDE IN THE SUNSHINE.

twinkly string lights

outdoor
ceiling fan

IDEAS FOR
CREATING A
COZY COASTAL
FEEL ON YOUR
PORCH

a table for
breakfast +
coffee

Wicker
furniture

an Adirondack
chair for reading

easy-to-clean rugs in
pretty patterns

neutral colors

lanterns for
ambient lighting

lots of potted
plants and
flowers

SMALL JOYS IN SPRINGTIME

- [ ] _____
- [ ] _____
- [ ] _____
- [ ] _____
- [ ] _____
- [ ] _____

ARE THERE TINY JOYS THAT YOU LOOK FORWARD TO EACH SEASON?

ADD YOUR FAVORITE SEASONAL JOYS TO EACH LIST.

SUMMER JOYS

_____
_____
_____
_____
_____
_____
_____
_____
_____
_____

fall favorites

THINGS THAT MAKE ME
HAPPY IN WINTER

THINGS

don't have to

BE PERFECT

for you to

FEEL JOY!

IF YOU FIND YOURSELF
PUTTING OFF JOY AND SAYING,
"I'LL BE HAPPY WHEN...,"
TRY ONE OF THESE PHRASES INSTEAD.

RIGHT IN THIS MOMENT, I CAN
BE HAPPY ABOUT

_____

_____

EVEN THOUGH I'M FEELING

_____

I STILL FEEL CONTENTMENT WHEN

_____

ACKNOWLEDGMENTS

Thank you to my amazing literary agent, Laurie Abkemeier, for the never-ending encouragement, thoughtful guidance, and invaluable advice. It's truly a joy to work with you, and I'll never stop feeling grateful for the day you found me! Thank you to my wonderful editor and fellow coastal grandmother, Patty Rice, for always being an incredible advocate of my work and for believing in my books. Thank you to everyone at Andrews McMeel Publishing for helping bring this book to life and for creating the best home for my universe of comfort! Thank you to my sister, Sarah Vaz, for the unconditional comfort and support. Thank you to my mom, Pat Vaz, for being the best cheerleader and for talking about my books to anyone who will listen—I'm so lucky to have you in my corner. And lastly, thank you to my darling husband, Joby Springsteen, for endlessly supporting me in everything I do, whether it's creating books or baking cakes. Life with you and Maizie is full of the sweetest joys.

Photo by Alice G. Patterson

ABOUT THE AUTHOR

Katie Vaz is an illustrator, author, designer, and hand-letterer based in Endicott, New York. Her previous books include *Don't Worry, Eat Cake: A Coloring Book to Help You Feel A Little Bit Better About Everything*; *Make Yourself Cozy: A Guide to Practicing Self-Care*; *The Escape Manual for Introverts*; *My Life in Plants: Flowers I've Loved, Herbs I've Grown, and Houseplants I've Killed on the Way to Finding Myself*; *Life with Plants: A Coloring Book*; and *Cottagecore Galore: A Timeless Coloring Book*. Her work has been featured on *ComicsBeat.com*, *IntrovertDear.com*, *BookRiot.com*, *ElephantJournal.com*, *Buzzfeed.com*, *RealSimple.com*, *WomansDay.com*, and *POPSUGAR.com*, and in *Stationery Trends* and *Time Out New York* magazines. Katie also designs her own line of greeting cards, prints, and other stationery products, which are sold both online and in brick-and-mortar shops across North America. She lives in upstate New York with her husband and daughter, their dog, Tater, and their cat, Kittenface.